Just a Face in the Crowd

By

Roger Horwood

This book is dedicated in memory of Dillon (2005 – 2017): without him these tales would never have seen the light of day

First published 2017

Cox Bank Publishing Limited
Coxbank, Audlem, CW3 0EU

Tel 01782 683000

email: info@coxbankpublishing.com

web: www.coxbankpublishing.com

ISBN 978-0-9956672-3-5

Front cover artwork by Foley Creative, Stoke-on-Trent

Cover design by Marketing Bi Design, Stoke-on-Trent

Printed and bound by Book Printing UK

CONTENTS

Roger Horwood

Born in Hartshill in the Potteries in 1941, it was when my parents moved to Woore in Shropshire and I attended the village junior school that my keen interest in football and cricket developed.

At work, I spent forty years in the ceramic tile industry, first as a sales clerk at H&R Johnson Tiles in Tunstall, then as a salesman for various tile companies travelling nationwide.

In 1986 my wife and I founded our own trade and retail tile company in Burton upon Trent. At the same time, I invited the whole of the nationwide tile industry to an exploratory meeting at the Belfry Hotel, Sutton Coldfield with a view to forming a national body to look after member's interests. The historic meeting took place on the 16 April 1986. I had a quiet word with the late and much respected Mr Trevor Howells of Craven Dunnill and Co Ltd of Bridgnorth, before the meeting commenced, and with over fifty companies in attendance, he kindly agreed to take the Chair. As a result, the National Association of Tile Distributors was formed that day.

What is now The Tile Association, with its Head Office in Stone in Staffordshire, embraces hundreds of members from manufacturing, distribution, retailing and tile-fixing sections in the UK and has strong connections with similar organisations overseas. Little did I realise back in 1986 that thirty-one years later the whole industry would have combined in this manner.

Having suffered a major heart attack in 1993, by 2000 my wife and I closed our business and retired.

I am a lifelong fan of Stoke City going back to the early 1950s and am a season ticket holder travelling to away matches as well when time permits.

My second love is cricket, and as far as that noble sport is concerned, I can never thank Woore Cricket Club enough from when I was a junior then a teenager and in my early twenties. It was there I learned how the game should be played, in a fiercely competitive, but just as importantly, sporting manner, a tradition which lasts to this day as our many rivals in the North Staffordshire and South Cheshire Cricket League will confirm.

After forty-five years away, due to work reasons, my wife and I returned to Woore Cricket Club, making the weekly round trip of eighty miles from our home in East Staffordshire to support them.

I have never forgotten my roots in the Potteries and surrounding area and I love being among my own people. Whether it is wandering around the cricket boundary with pals from both teams, or cheering the Potters on at home or away this is where my heart will always be.

"Cos they kick a bau agen a wall til it bosts?"

Proud to be a Potter, and equally proud to be an Ambassador for the Sir Stanley Matthews Coaching Foundation.

Foreword

As a former Sports Reporter on the old City Times newspaper in the early sixties, when I was in my early twenties, I used to love submitting my reports to the Editor and seeing them published in this weekly paper. Unfortunately, one day I had better things to do than attend a dull council meeting at Kidsgrove and so got the sack. But I never lost my enjoyment for telling tales by using the written word.

Having travelled extensively throughout the UK for twenty years, and lived in the Potteries, North Shropshire, North Cheshire and East Staffordshire inevitably I picked up many sporting stories and football fans banter. These are some of them.

How they came to be published in a book is a bit of a story in itself...

A SHAGGY DOG TALE

A pal of mine at St Georges Park, the National Football Centre near Burton upon Trent, was the owner of a handsome dog named Dillon. Along with Dillon's owner, my wife and I are members of the Health Club which is on site in the Hilton Hotel. An elderly lady who originates from Leek also became a member of the Health Club, and unknown to me, word had got round that she was a very talented artist.

Over coffee one morning I noticed my pal was admiring a photo of his dog Dillon.

"What a smashing photo", I said, "it's super".

"Rog" he said, "it's a painting", to which I responded, "It can't be".

But it was - and it turned out the artist was in great demand to paint other members' pets.

When a relative passed away many years ago in May Bank in Newcastle-under-Lyme the family came across an old autographed postcard of Sir Stanley Matthews and because of my strong support for Stoke City the family offered it to me.

It was taken in 1936 when the great man had been awarded his fourth international cap for England against Scotland at Hampden Park. The attendance at that match is the British record: 149,000 spectators! Sir Stanley Matthews was my hero and I was honoured to see him play when he returned to Stoke City in 1961.

And yes, you've guessed, I persuaded the elderly lady to paint a copy. The painting is stunning and is now in the possession of Sir Stan's daughter Jean Gough. It has been donated by the artist and will be sold at auction in due course.

As a result of meeting Jean, I have become an enthusiastic supporter of the Sir Stanley Matthews Coaching Foundation. It suddenly dawned on me that I might be able to help to raise money for the Foundation by writing a book. I have always enjoyed writing and telling stories.

Jean had already seen a couple of articles I had written about Sir Stan, and kindly mentioned them to Peter Hooper of Cox Bank Publishing.

Following a chat with Peter and with his encouragement *Just a Face in the Crowd* has become reality.

It's taken me all winter of 2016-17 to write my memories, working largely in the peace and quiet of the beautiful island of Madeira. But I only missed four games at the bet365.

It contains a selection of 45 tales from the 70-plus I ended up writing, dating back to 1953.

And all because of a dog named Dillon!!!

The tales are mainly true recollections of Stoke City, football banter from Manchester, Liverpool, Birmingham, Derby, and of course the Potteries.

To say I have enjoyed telling my tales is an understatement, I've loved every minute of it. It's been a huge task, but at the age of 75 it has kept my brain alert. Retirement is wonderful, but at times it can get a little boring!

My grateful thanks to my wife for putting up with me whilst lost in my own world of memories, and to the encouragement given to me by Jean and by Anthony Bunn, Editor of the Stoke City Fanzine *Duck*, who has previously published a selection of my stories in his magazine.

A short disclaimer: these tales (and the retelling of a favourite joke and anecdote or two) are very much my personal memories: I've recorded events as best as I can recall them, but I'm very aware that everyone remembers matches and events differently. Any errors are mine and are unintentional; and none of the tales is intended to cause offence - they are just memories and recollections of a life lived in the crowd. I hope you enjoy them.

Roger Horwood

Stanley Matthews

Painting by Muriel Valentine, from an original photograph on the occasion of his 4th England cap.

1. Relegated by the Rams. 25 April 1953

This was the first match I can remember.

I stood out in the open on the Stoke End of the Victoria Ground and witnessed Stoke City's relegation to Division Two. In those days, Campbell Tiles had their factory just across the way and fans used to say they lit the kilns in order to coincide with the kick off, so that smoke from them would envelop the ground and put the opposition off.

Yes, there was smoke that day but it didn't do us any good. Derby County were already down and we had to win. Simple as that. A draw was no good. Unfortunately, at a critical stage of the game we missed a penalty - and we were done for. The Skipper, Big Kenny Thomson, a powerful Scottish centre half in the Denis Smith mould overruled our normal penalty taker Frankie Mountford and took it himself. As Captain, he felt he had to take responsibility. The argument rages to this day as to what happened. Did Kenny hit the bar? Hit one of the posts? Shoot wide? Or did the goalie save it? I think he shot over the bar.

But you need to be at least seventy-five years old like me to remember.

2. The Unofficial Champions of Europe

In the 1950s, Wolverhampton Wanderers under their stern and dictatorial manager Stan Cullis were blessed with a superb team, carrying all before them and winning the old First Division in 1953-4. However, this was not enough for the Wolves Board and Manager who wanted to compete with and beat the best teams in Europe.

The Wolves had a 'nursery team' affiliated to them at Donnington in Shropshire where there was and still is a major British Army base. Several of the day boys at Adams Grammar School in Newport, Salop, where I was a boarder played for them at various age levels. The team was called Donnington Swifts, and the best players hoped to get a chance to sign for the most feared team in England at that time: The Wolves.

Soccer was banned at Adams, rugby being the only permitted Winter ball game. It made no difference however to many of the soccer-mad pupils, and as soon as the teachers were out of sight, a football was produced from nowhere.

The school, as with many other grammar schools at the time, considered soccer a game not suitable for the superior image they were trying to create and so, like it or not, we were obliged to play a game where the bigger you had developed as a youngster, inevitably the more effective you were. The smaller pupils, many of whom were quite skilful with a rugby ball or football, did not have the physical strength to compete and were, like myself, subjected to brutal tackling. Whenever we managed to play an unauthorised game of football we, the smaller boys with our superior ball control, were much the better performers.

When we learned the mighty Wolves had arranged two friendly matches against the Russian Champions, Spartak Moscow, and Honved Budapest, the Hungarian Champions, acknowledged to be probably the best team in Northern Europe, we were clamouring for tickets, and because of the day boys' connection with Donnington Swifts they were duly secured. Molineux was under twenty miles away.

The Headmaster and teachers were powerless to stop the day boys from attending, but because of the bigoted attitude of the school towards soccer, the boarders were barred from going. Inevitably, those boarders who had managed to get tickets for both games attended anyway. On both occasions, on our return, because in the School's view we had left the premises without permission and attended football matches, we were severely caned by an unforgiving Headmaster.

In the first match on 16th November 1954 Spartak Moscow were destroyed 4-0; and in the game against Honved, Budapest on 13th December 1954, Wolves won again, this time 3-2. Both matches were played in front of over 55,000 spectators under floodlights: at that time a fairly new innovation, and were televised live. Incidentally, both games featured the Stoke-born inside forward and free-scoring English International Dennis Wilshaw, who went on to play for Stoke in the late fifties until around the time Stanley Matthews came home.

After the two matches Stan Cullis announced to the world that "The Wolves are unofficial Champions of Europe". Such had been the worldwide interest in the matches, the following season the European Cup was born.

But although I was pleased for my pals from Donnington that their team had done so well, my heart was still with my home team, Stoke City. At every opportunity, usually with a couple of other boarders who were also Stoke fans, I attended Stoke's home games by going AWOL, bringing the inevitable flogging on my return. We got to matches by steam train from Newport Station (no longer in existence) to Stafford, then caught the steam train to Stoke. The fact I was selected as the school's second team scrum half at rugby didn't make any difference. I still went to Stoke games and to hell with the consequences.

When the then League champions Chelsea entered the European Cup competition in 1954-5, the backward-thinking Blazers at the FA banned them from taking part and the reign of Real Madrid began, who went on to win the title for six years on the trot. The following season Manchester United were English First Division Champions and their Board of Directors and Manager Matt Busby (later Sir Matt) told the FA they were entering and nothing was going to stop them. And so, the legendary "Busby Babes" were born, only to be cruelly crippled in the fateful Munich air disaster on 6 February 1958 when eight of United's highly promising young team died.

It was because of Munich and the way the club rose from the dead and gained massive worldwide support that Manchester United have such a huge fan base today, many of whom don't live anywhere near Old Trafford. That was the rebirth of the club as we know it today.

3. An All Time Record

On 25 February 1957, as usual I caught the steam train from my boarding school in Newport, Shropshire to watch the Potters play Lincoln City in a Second Division match at the Victoria Ground. I stood on the Boothen End with a pal of mine from school.

What unfolded that afternoon is a record performance by a winger that stands to this day. Tim Coleman scored seven goals, yes SEVEN in one match as we pulverised the opposition.

Over the last few years at cricket matches at Weston and Crewe following my team Woore often I've had a chat with former Stoke player Johnny King, a very popular performer with the fans who was playing that day. Johnny remembers the game well as he scored the other goal and always maintains Tim missed his easiest chance and should have scored eight.

This really was a once in a lifetime performance by an unexceptional but hard working professional footballer. Will any winger ever break his record?

4. The Decade Without Stanley Matthews

Stanley Matthews left Stoke City for Blackpool in 1947. I cannot recall the first time I saw him, but am told by relatives that my late Father took me to see him play at the Victoria Ground when I was six years old. He carried me on his shoulders because the Maestro was already over thirty years of age and I might have never got the chance to see him perform again.

My first recollection of seeing him was on a tiny black and white television set in the 1953-4 Cup Final against Bolton Wanderers. Blackpool won 4-3, Stan had a "blinder" and to this day the game is known as 'The Matthews Final'. By then of course Stoke had been relegated, and despite a few optimistic seasons spread over the 1950s when we thought we might win promotion, we never achieved it.

Every now and then a rumour would fly around the Potteries that Stan was coming home. But it never happened until the eventful days of October 1961. On the 14th October 1961 we played Preston North End in a routine Division Two game. Stoke were going nowhere, the gate was a pathetic 8,409 and the fans like me were really down in the dumps.

And then the news broke!! Stan's coming home.

And he did, and in front of 35,974 yes – THIRTY-FIVE THOUSAND NINE HUNDRED AND SEVENTY-FOUR fans - played his first match against Huddersfield Town on 28th October 1961.

We won, with the mere presence of Stan, who didn't do a lot that day, putting the fear of God into the opposition. At 46 years of age the 'Wizard of the Dribble' had cast his spell and 35,974 fans were in raptures. The Press were agog at this fairy tale home-coming and so was the whole area and indeed every football fan in the country.
From memory, the then new Boothen Stand had just about been completed, and for his homecoming match I was able to jump onto the windowsill of a room right behind me in the Boothen Paddock. This I

think was one of the new unfinished dressing rooms. Across the other side on the Butler Street side was a huge banner.

It said quite simply, "Welcome home Stan - THANKS A MILLION"

5. Stoke's 12th Man

This anecdote may or may not have happened exactly as told, but I like to think that it reflects the love and respect that Stoke-on-Trent held for its greatest football hero.

When Stanley Matthews came home in October 1961 he was 46 years old and clearly needed to be careful about the type of surface he played on in case he got clattered. The Manager Tony Waddington was aware of this, so forty-eight hours before Stan's first home game against Huddersfield Town in October 1961 he and Stan conducted a pitch inspection.

There had been a particularly dry Autumn and the pitch was very, very hard.

"What do you reckon Stan?" Tony asked the Great Man.

"Bit dicey this, too hard, don't fancy playing on this" he said.

"There's not a lot I can do about it" Tony replied.

Stan, quick as a flash, responded "Well I can. I've got some pals in the Fire Brigade. I was at school with them. I'll have a quiet word. They are all Stoke fans."

Waddo said "You can't do that Stan." And Stan said "Oh yes we can. There's nothing in the League rules to say we can't"

Who got in touch with the Fire Brigade remains a mystery, but on the Friday night before the match a City of Stoke-on-Trent appliance arrived with the firemen and gave the pitch a three-hour drenching.

When the ref arrived for his customary 10.00am inspection that morning he was astonished. "Good grief " he said. "Bit wet, isn't it? We've had no rain for weeks".

"Localised downpour ref" the groundsman responded in deadpan fashion.

Stan of course, because of his balance and nimble footwork, was totally at ease whereas his opponents were all over the place.

Thereafter the clandestine waterings were a regular feature for our home matches when Stan was playing.

Stoke fans should always be grateful to the City of Stoke-on-Trent Fire Brigade. They really were Stoke's 12th Man.

6. Shunted up a Siding in Leicester. 10 Jan 1962

Stanley Matthews had come home and there was huge interest in Stoke City's 3rd Round FA Cup tie at Filbert Street against Leicester City. The gate of over 35,500 included several thousand Stoke fans, many of whom had travelled by Football Specials, steam trains in those days starting from Congleton and picking up along the way at Kidsgrove, Longport, Etruria, Stoke and Longton stations.

We earned a 1-1 draw on this Saturday afternoon game, and then the problems started for the train I was on. We were shunted up a siding in Leicester and left there for hours. The train eventually got back to the Potteries after midnight, and when it got to Longton we were asked to get off by the guards as the line was closed to Stoke Station and onwards due to maintenance. To cap it all, Longton Station was locked up and we couldn't get out.

Hundreds of fans then made their way along the line and eventually when we had arrived at Stoke Station we managed to get out as there were night staff on duty. They were amazed at the scene of us legging it along the line towards them. Incidentally, we saw no sign of maintenance work taking place along the route, and to this day have no idea what had caused this fiasco, from being shunted up the siding to being turfed off at Longton.

All finished well however, because on 15 January 1962 in front of 38,515 fans we won the replay 5-2.

I sat in the Butler Street corner stand at the Victoria Ground that night with a young lady who became my wife in 1966, and who never ceases to remind me - after over 50 years - that football and Stoke City seem always to come first!!

7. Accrington Stanley's Last Stand. 2 March 1962

Pat Connolly who had previously been playing for Knutton Village Hall in, I think, the Newcastle and District League in North Staffordshire got his big chance when he made his debut for Crewe Alexandra as a professional footballer against Accrington Stanley at Gresty Road on this Friday evening game under floodlights.

It was played in blizzard conditions and the Alex won 4-0. I cannot remember if Pat scored.

My pals and I had gone to the game as we knew Pat through the Crystal Ballroom in Newcastle and we were shocked when on the following Monday Accrington Stanley went out of business and resigned from the league having completed only 33 of their scheduled 46 matches. Their record was expunged.

Although the Club reformed in 1968, it was 2005 and 43 long years before they were promoted back to the Football League.

Accrington, along with the Potters, were of course founder members of the League.

8. Stoke-on-Trent Schoolboys Win the Cup

It was May 1962 and the best Stoke-on-Trent Schoolboys Team we had been blessed with for some time played the away leg of the English Schools Trophy Cup Final at Anfield.

The first leg had been played at Vale Park with a large crowd being present. The old Wolves and Stoke City goal-scoring forward Dennis Wilshaw, who was also a schoolmaster and Potteries born, managed the team.

A sizeable following from our area, including a few friends of mine, made the journey up to Anfield. We won the game, won the Trophy and the team proudly took it home.

As I recall, in that side that day were two players who went on to play for Stoke City: full back Bill Bentley and centre forward John Woodward. Both played first team football for us. How many of that team signed and played for the Vale and other clubs I don't know.

Staggeringly though, I believe the attendance at Anfield that night was 49,000!!! For a Schools Cup Final. Quite incredible, I'm sure you will agree.

But of course, it took place at the early days of the arrival of Liverpool back in the First Division, with the inspirational Scots Manager Bill Shankly creating a massive Football Fever on Merseyside. And that's not forgetting their local rivals Everton, who also were very strongly supported as well.

9. Club Office Chaos

When Stanley Matthews returned to Stoke City in 1961 and we won promotion the following season, I was roped in by a relative who worked part-time in the Club Office to help out with season ticket sales. The fact that the office was inundated with applications says it all. The place was in turmoil. There were notes and coins of the realm everywhere. I even found notes in the office loos. But no, we didn't!!!

Come the opening match against Spurs when my father and I arrived to take our seats by the Directors' Box we found, as did dozens of other fans in that area, ours already occupied. In the bedlam that had taken place in the Office we had inadvertently double sold them.

How it was all sorted out I can't remember, but it was and everyone went home happy because we won 2-1...

10. "Show Your Class Dennis"

There must have been a very good reason why the City of Stoke-on-Trent chose to name a road by the bet365 Stadium after Dennis Viollet. And there certainly was. When Stoke City Manager Tony Waddington snapped him up from Manchester United in 1962 Dennis left behind him his United record of most league goals in a season – 32 - a record that stands to this day. Dennis was a survivor of the horrific Munich air disaster on the 6th February 1958 when eight of his fellow players known as the "Busby Babes" perished.

Waddo quickly realised Dennis could be of more value to the team playing a bit deeper and bringing the ball through and he was so right. Dennis oozed quality. With his jet-black hair, slim build and lightening pace, to see him darting through the middle with the ball like a knife through butter was to see real class. And often his straight dashes resulted in a searing 20-yard shot on goal. 66 goals in 207 matches from this position told its own story to us.

In addition, he had the vision to split defences with deadly accurate side-footed through-balls which only really talented players possess. And he could also 'put his foot in where it hurts' if required to do so.

As a regular penalty taker, Dennis would normally aim very hard at goal, so if the goalie got anywhere near it the sheer speed of the ball would do the trick. But one day he decided "to educate" the Boothen End on how a penalty should really be taken. So, to show them and the rest of us how it should be done he attempted to pass it side-footed into the net. It was very carefully taken as you would expect but unfortunately the ball wasn't moving at any pace, and the flipping goalie saved it. Dennis was crestfallen!!

A few weeks later we got another penalty, again at the Boothen End, and as usual, Dennis carefully placed the ball on the spot. The next thing we knew was Big John Ritchie shoving him out of the way, getting the okay from the ref and blasting it, and I mean blasting the ball so hard it nearly burst the back of the net. "Big John" stood there, hands on hips admiring his effort and looking at a rather sheepish Dennis. "Now that's how to take a penalty " the Big Man said.

In the Boothen Stand where I used to sit with my father, the gentleman who sat next to us, from memory a butcher from Nantwich named Mr Welch, had a favourite saying: "Show your Class, Dennis, show your Class". That summed up one of the silkiest and most elegant players we have been lucky enough to have on our books.

"Show your Class Dennis, show your Class". And in five seasons with us he certainly did!!

11. A Foggy Farce in the Early '60s

It was a league match in the early Sixties between Stoke City and Swansea Town (as they were known back then) and we were all stunned when the ref decided to start the game. A blanket of fog covered the Victoria Ground making playing conditions nigh on impossible. After a few minutes, the ball arrived at the feet of Eddie "Chopper" Clamp, the Stoke wing half. I was in the Boothen Paddock on the half way line right by where Chopper was on the touch line. The Boothen End and most spectators had no idea where the ball was because the fog was so dense.

To hoots of laughter from those who could see Chopper picked the ball up, put it under his arm and ran down the wing towards the Stoke End, rugby style. He then put it down and centred it with his foot. Those who could see through the fog on the Stoke End said the Swansea goalie managed to spot the ball, and hoofed it down the pitch where it disappeared into the murk. The ref had no idea what had happened but could hear those few fans who had seen what Chopper had done chortling their heads off.

The rest of the ground and linesman on that side hadn't seen it either. It was clear to the ref that some tomfoolery had been taking place and he then abandoned the match.

Purely from a hard-tackling aspect Chopper made Norman Hunter look like a choir boy.

12. Back Where We Belong

As the season of 1962-3 progressed it was becoming clear Tony Waddington had built a team capable of taking Stoke City back to the First Division. With a backbone of very experienced players, and of course the presence of Stanley Matthews back in his red and white shirt, the fans became increasingly confident. Easter 1963 is my most memorable period that season.

Good Friday, 12 April, 62,138 at Sunderland's Roker Park saw us come away with a 0-0 draw. The very next day, Easter Saturday, we beat Cardiff City 1-0 in front of 30,419 at home and then 48 hours later, our third game in four days, on Easter Monday 42,366 packed into the Victoria Ground to see us triumph over Sunderland 2-1. We were well and truly on the way.

A few weeks later, an estimated 12,000 Stoke fans charged up to Bury for an evening game. Many left work early, some just took a day off without pay. But we got there. There was traffic chaos at 6.30pm that night in the area, so much so that many Stoke fans abandoned their cars in one huge traffic jam and marched off to Gigg Lane. A couple of young police officers decided to start issuing tickets for illegal parking, which they put on our cars but they rapidly ran out of the appropriate forms. Fortunately, a senior police officer arrived and said to the young officers "Steady on lads. If this was your team you wouldn't be doing this would you?" Common sense prevailed and the tickets were removed.

We lost the game and Stan didn't play. A staggering 66,199 was the attendance at Stamford Bridge around this time, with many Londoners attending the Stoke match because they thought they might never see Stan play in the Capital again. The sheer pulling power of the Maestro was unbelievable. Is this the biggest ever attendance for a Second Division match on a club ground?

And then on an emotional Saturday, 18th May against Luton Town 33,644 fans saw our dream come true. Promotion back into the big time.

The second oldest league club in the world had made it, and make no mistake our hero from 'up Hanley' had made it all possible. The roof came off the Boothen End when Stan scored the goal that did the damage.

I was standing in the Butler Street Paddock on the half way line. Jimmy McIlroy received the ball on the wing by me and spotted Stan flying down the right wing on the Boothen Paddock side. He had started his run just inside his own half. He had ghosted down the wing unmarked. Jimmy's incredible cross-field ball from one side of the pitch to the other landed just in front of Stan, who cut in, skipped round the goalie and planted the ball in the back of the Boothen End net. You couldn't have written this. No-one could.

I have never seen so many Stokies in tears. That ball from Jimmy to Stan will remain with me forever. It was sheer telepathy between two wonderful players. The immortal Stanley Matthews, at the time the greatest footballer the world had ever seen, had paid his debt to the Club that had given him his chance, and rewarded his own people for their support dating back to the 1930s.

Sir Stan we salute you!

13. Snowballed at Anfield

Three of us, all Stoke fans, managed to get tickets for the European Cup tie at Anfield on 17 March 1964 when Liverpool played FC Cologne, the West German champions.

As we left the Potteries for this night-time match it was already snowing, and as we approached Merseyside it had become very heavy. Nevertheless, fans were admitted to the Stadium and well before the scheduled kick off there over 50,000 present, including over 22,000 on the Kop up to their normal boisterous mischievous antics.

We were in one of the Paddocks and as typical at Anfield packed in so tightly we could hardly get a fag packet out of our pockets. We were of course standing. With the Kop bellowing out in unison "ee-I-Addio-we won the war", the tiny figure of Liverpool Manager Bill Shankly waded onto the pitch with the snow by this time up to his knees. His thumbs down said it all.

Over the tannoy an announcement was made that if everyone was patient fans would be given a ticket for the rearranged match date before they left, and we all duly got one. This was the signal for the Kop to take over proceedings as hundreds of young fans poured off it to invade the pitch and start a giant snowball fight.

"Pa....a...ddocks, Pa...a...ddocks, Pa...a...ddocks!" the Kop chanted. The youngsters lined up in military precision, and an elderly fella with a walking stick raised it up, and as he lowered it the Kop shouted "Fire!". And that was it. We were absolutely bombarded and drenched because we were so tightly packed in we couldn't get out of the way.

But we got our own back and chanted "Now the Kop, Now the Kop!" and they too got the full treatment. And then a moment I shall never forget.

The Kop all standing, yes over 22,000 of them swaying side-to-side with their red and white scarves stretched out horizontally above their heads, and flags and banners flying, with the heavy snow tumbling

30

down, burst into the world's most famous football anthem. It was the first time I had heard it sung live as it was then a fairly new rendering. My whole body was tingling and it brought tears to my eyes as 'You'll Never Walk Alone' was sung with enormous passion by the Kop and then by the entire stadium.

We got home in the middle of the night because of the heavy snow. I think it took us around seven hours. But drenched to the skin, we were still laughing at the snowball scrap and highly emotional too, after the unforgettable scenes and the singing on the Kop.

14. Georgie Best

In 1963 George Best burst on the scene with Manchester United and within months became a superstar, with a worldwide following both male and female. He became known as "the fifth Beatle", such was his appeal to young people.

When he built his own home in leafy north Cheshire four years later, the queue to supply free-of-charge construction materials and interior finishes from businesses anxious for Georgie to endorse their products was unbelievable. The general consensus was he got his ultra-modern home built for nothing!!! How on earth it got passed the planning authority I don't know. The property resembled a Hollywood style abode. It stuck out like a sore thumb in such a reserved area. The exterior was clad, from memory, in shiny white wall tiles and it really did resemble something from outer space. It was open plan with large windows and no fence, so people unfortunately could look in and 'have a nose'.

Word got around quickly and soon the road outside was invaded by teenage girls who sometimes hired coaches to bring them straight from school. They would stand outside just hoping for a glimpse of their idol. I often came home from work that way to our house in Poynton and was amazed at the scenes.

One lovely spring morning I was shuffling some papers in H&R Johnson Tiles' regional office in Pall Mall, off Market Street in Manchester City Centre. Normally the female members of staff would pop out and fetch the lunch sandwiches at around 12.00 noon, but on this particular day they told the manager there was an urgent parcel to collect from the Post Office. So, the boss advised them to fetch it and the sandwiches as well straight away. A few minutes later we heard shrill screams coming from outside. The whole area was choc-a-bloc with young ladies going absolutely crazy: Georgie and his pal, legendary Manchester City player Mike Summerbee, were opening their new boutique "Edwardia". The offices in the city centre came to a standstill.

Everywhere Georgie went he was the centre of attraction. He was living in a goldfish bowl. He really was the player who started the show business era for footballers. With his jet-black long flowing hair, socks around his ankles, jinking his way round two and sometimes three defenders, often on mud heaps, his ball control was a joy to watch. Even we "Stokies" had to admire him, though he nearly drove us daft.

Georgie though was no innocent when things got tough and he could certainly mix it if anyone tried to tackle him in a crude fashion. Big Jack Charlton, an England World Cup winner in 1966, one of the hardest centre halves in the game and part of the famous Leeds United team, had decided to keep a little black book of opponents he felt were owed one. Georgie was the first name in it!!! The sight of lanky Jack, eyes blazing, and intent on retribution chasing the impish fleeing Georgie around the pitch after a confrontation will live in the memory of those who saw it.

Belfast Airport - the George Best Belfast City Airport - is a fitting tribute to Northern Ireland's favourite son. The wonderfully talented genius and lovable lad from the back streets of that great city, who with his warm Irish accent charmed everyone he met, lived life a bit too much to the full and tragically passed away at too young an age. We who can remember him will never see his like again.

Everlasting Georgie, forever in our hearts whichever club we follow.

15. Needles and Pins

Manchester City v Stoke City 1964, League Cup semi-final second leg.

The cavernous Maine Road stadium was three quarters empty with only around 16,000 present, including around 500 Stokies for this match. This ground had held over 84,000 in 1934 when Man City played us in a FA Cup tie. My late Father-in-law along with over 20,000 Stoke supporters attended and got there mainly by steam trains.

This 1964 cup game was in the infancy of the League Cup and there was a general lack of interest in this tournament as the FA Cup was the only one that mattered back then.

We lost 1-0, but went through to the final on aggregate in the two-legged fixture. We lost the final – I saw both games home and away – 3-2 I think, on aggregate. One thing I can never forget: booming over the tannoy system at Maine Road echoed one of the most famous songs of the Mersey Sound: "Needles and Pins" by The Searchers. I think it had only been released a few days earlier. I can still hear it today and remember the banter with their fans as in those days there was no segregation.

Can anyone else remember those matches and the friendship that existed between supporters of both clubs? The handshakes at the end and always the words "See you next season mate, same spot".

And sure enough we did.

16. The Sale of "Big John"- Season 1966

Other than the uproar in Stoke-on-Trent when Stanley Matthews asked to leave the club in 1938, which was before I was born, I can never remember such a united outcry against the Directors and Manager Tony Waddington as when "Big John" Ritchie was sold to Sheffield Wednesday in 1966.

When I got home from work and picked the Sentinel up I could not believe what I was reading. My mind went numb. Surely this can't be true? The Sentinel's made a mistake. But they hadn't and the club had sold the best centre forward we'd signed since Freddie Steele.

He had already scored four goals against Wednesday in one game and a hat-trick in another. No wonder they were keen to get their hands on him!!

Big John, a strongly built and forceful centre forward was born to be a goal scorer. Yes, he missed some chances as all great centre forwards do, but he was also always in the danger area and in there for the half chance. Unfortunately, some of the 'know-alls' in the Directors Box and on the Boothen End expected a powerful and very strong header of the ball to be just like Stan and also have the ability and twinkle toes with the ball at his feet.

If our idol had been born with that sort of ability, you would have been made to break the bank to buy him. Word spread like wildfire round the Potteries of this crazy decision by the Board and Manager. We know from bitter experience that Stoke used to have a reputation as a selling Club.

Thank goodness those days have changed. Letters from irate fans inundated the Evening Sentinel for day after day, and then to crown it all, John Woodward, a very promising young striker who was banging them in in the reserves was transferred to Aston Villa a few weeks later.

From what looked like being a top five place our season was wrecked as the club's goal-scoring machines left. It all boiled over when

Wednesday came to Stoke in a League Game and beat us. I think the Big Man might have scored as well, just to rub it in.

It is over fifty years ago so the memory fades a little, but I do recall after this match angry fans' tempers boiling over and stones being thrown at the Boardroom windows. What had promised to be a really good season for us finished in disappointment and with thousands of fans disconsolate.

Two years later the Board and Tony Waddington realised their mistake and Big John came home to the club who had originally signed him from non-League Kettering Town. After scoring many, many more goals for us he became our all-time leading scorer.

The bust of John Ritchie outside the Boothen End is a fitting tribute to a player who will forever be in the hearts of those who saw him play. If only he was leading the line for us today and banging them in.

17. Denis Smith - The Iron Man. Stoke City '68-'82

Denis Smith, born in the Meir, in the Potteries, was one of football's strongest and most powerful players and he paid for it with injuries galore. Despite five broken legs, four broken noses, collar-bones, ankles, fingers and toes he somehow managed to put in four hundred and ninety-three appearances for Stoke City before ending his career with a spell at York City in the lower leagues.

During those years with us he was the true heartbeat of Stoke City, always leading from the front and playing as an out-and-out Centre Half commanding the penalty area. On the terrible muddy pitches, or the bumpy rock-hard frost-bitten ones, Denis never changed his uncompromising way of playing. Whether towering above everyone to head the ball clear of the danger area or saving the situation with a fantastic last-ditch sliding tackle, he really was one of the most feared defenders in the old First Division.

Some of the Iron Man's tackles were made without any consideration for his own well-being. He just went in there and did what had to be done. I honestly think opposition players baulked at the prospect of coming up against him. The whole of the Boothen End at the Victoria Ground used to shudder at some of his obliterating tackles.

For my generation, he was our talisman. A Stokie born and bred, playing for his home city team.

When he packed up playing he went into management with York City, Sunderland (a massive job), Bristol City, Oxford United and then finally Wrexham. During those years away from home he amassed over one thousand matches as a manager, joining an exclusive club including of course our former Boss Tony Pulis.

Today, when we get into our cars after the game at the bet365 Stadium there is one person on local radio we listen to above all others. When the Iron Man speaks, the Potteries listen!!

18. Queuing Up for Cup Tickets. Early '70s

It was an exciting time to be a Stoke City fan in the early seventies. Possibly the finest team the club had assembled since 1947 - when we nearly won the old First Division - reached two FA Cup semi-finals against the Arsenal. We lost both after controversial refereeing decisions in two replays, but we did win the League Cup in 1972, beating Chelsea.

In those days, mainly because of financial constraints, many fans could ill-afford season tickets, so when it came to these massive games the only way to get a ticket was to queue up all night. And boy oh boy, what an experience it was!!!

Because most grounds had mainly standing areas, the really large ones like Hillsborough, Villa Park, Old Trafford, and Goodison Park, where these games were played meant well over 25,000 tickets went on sale at the Victoria Ground for each one. Tickets were normally sold on a Sunday morning at 10.00am, so it meant a minimum sixteen hours, yes 16 HOURS', wait.

Queues started to form straight after the Saturday match at 5.00pm if we were at home and by 7pm there were up to 25,000 fans waiting, often in bitterly cold, wet and windy weather. The queue had already stretched nearly all the way round the ground by 10.00pm which is when 'chucking out' time was in those days. Fans would arrive having had one too many and try to gate crash the front. To cries of "Aye you, back of the queue, aye you, back of the queue" inevitably scuffles broke out but the City of Stoke-on-Trent police officers with assistance from their four legged friends generally sorted it all out in an amicable way.

By midnight the queue was four or five deep round the ground, with those at the rear wondering if they were too late and would not get a ticket. Family and friends of many fans bought blankets, heating equipment and chairs to make the night a little more comfortable. Bonfires were lit as well, glowing in the dark particularly on the Butler Street Side where the conditions underfoot were diabolical.

Toilet facilities were non-existent. We, the fans were left to it.

All night we waited, singing the pop songs of the day. I distinctly remember "Rose Garden" being a hit at the time.

However, to much infuriation, the Club, despite seeing the huge mass of people waiting patiently, refused to commence selling until the scheduled time of 10.00am. That did not go down at all well, but we just had to put up with it. I obtained my precious tickets for the games normally around 11.00am, often frozen, wet, and bursting for a "Jimmy Riddle". Was it worth the wait? Of course it was.

Today, at the bet365 Stadium, undoubtedly one of the coldest grounds in the country, can you imagine a queue all the way round the ground four or five deep with the normal howling gale blowing? The prospect of waiting there for at least sixteen hours and overnight doesn't bear thinking about.

Heartbreak and Happiness following the Potters.

19. Banksy's Horror Story

During his career with Chesterfield, Leicester City, and Stoke City, 'Banks of England' - as he was known to the press and the fans - made many great saves. The impossible one against Pele in the World Cup of 1970; the incredible one at the Boleyn Ground, when he tipped over Geoff Hurst's thunderbolt penalty to keep us in the League Cup in the early Seventies, which of course we went on to win at Wembley; and many, many more.

It was at Hillsborough, in the final moments of a FA Cup Semi Final against the Arsenal on 22 March 1971, in front of over 54,000 spectators, that a first ever Cup Final appearance was denied us. Gordon comfortably collected a loose ball but an Arsenal player dislodged the ball from his hands. Every Stoke fan behind the incident at the infamous Leppings Lane knew it was a clear foul and waited for it to be awarded. To our utter disbelief, as the ball trickled over the goal line outside the post the ref awarded a corner.

25,000 Stoke fans were incandescent at this dreadful decision but we were powerless to do anything about it despite the outraged protests of our players. In came the corner, a Stoke player, John Mahoney handled it and correctly a penalty was awarded - and the rest is history.

We lost the replay at the Villa a few days later 2-0 in front of over 62,000 and the dream was over.

Today there is no doubt that the Arsenal player involved with the incident at Hillsborough should have been penalised. But it was the arrogant way in which the Arsenal players celebrated in front of us that caused the hostility towards that club which as we all know persists to this day.

They knew they'd got away with a 2-2 draw thanks to a blunder by the ref. There used to be a saying about the Arsenal 50 years ago as they regularly used to win matches 1-0. LUCKY ARSENAL - and they certainly were that day.

My wife was having a "clear out" under the staircase recently and chucked out all my old football books and put them in the garage. I rummaged through them and found, attached by Sellotape to one of them, my ticket for the semi-final at Hillsborough, March 1971 against the Arsenal. Number 7843. Price 60p. YES, SIXTY PENCE.

20. Bobby Charlton's Testimonial Match. 18 Sept 1972

The first football special trains from Glasgow Central pulled into Manchester Victoria Railway Station at 10.00am.

They were carrying thousands of fanatical Glasgow Celtic fans whose club had been invited to play Manchester United in a testimonial game for Bobby Charlton. From memory, the kick off was scheduled for around 7.30pm.

And that was great news for the landlords of the pubs in Manchester City Centre, but not so good for people shopping or working in the area. I don't think I have ever seen so many tam o'shanters and kilts in one place in my life. To describe the atmosphere as raucous was an understatement.

Remember, all those years ago Celtic had been the first British Club to win the European Cup in 1967. I watched that match on TV in black and white at home, and to any football fan it was truly unforgettable. That team is known to this day as the 'Lisbon Lions". Lisbon was the city in which the game was played against the ultra-defensive Italian team Internazionale of Milan.

Lisbon is allegedly also the city with more direct descendants of Glaswegians than any other in Europe, as many fans stayed and never returned home, reliving their dream victory every day for the rest of their lives!

By lunchtime Manchester City centre was awash with fans in the green and white hooped shirts. They drunk the place dry and all the famous Celtic songs, many of Irish origin were being sung. It was a giant party. My firm's office was in the middle of it. Through the window I witnessed it all. But there was no trouble, no fighting, no abuse, just good-natured banter which the Scots are known for worldwide.

That afternoon I had an appointment in Preston at 2.30pm so I had plenty of time to get back for the match. When I hit the M6 the sight was unbelievable. Pouring southbound were Glasgow Co-op milk carts, dustbin lorries, the odd ambulance and even a hearse. They were all packed with Celtic fans. The Scottish flag was flying from them and of course the Celtic banners. This was an invasion by fans of a huge club with worldwide support.

The match was of course even more significant because both teams had by then won the European Cup, United triumphing in 1968 at Wembley.

And so to the match which was attended by over 60,000 fans paying tribute to Bobby. At the time, the largest ever attendance for a testimonial match. Talk about a friendly!!

Some estimated there were close on 30,000 Celtic fans present. The two teams had no choice, despite it being classed as a friendly, to go at each other hell for leather. How on earth it finished with no goals being scored I don't know.

But that night three great Scottish Players were on the pitch, the King of Old Trafford Denis Law, playing for United and another famous United player who joined them later, Lou Macari now an adopted Stokie of course, and finally, the one and only Celtic and Liverpool idol, Kenny Dalglish. What would they be worth today?

As we left the ground my pals and I walked over the Warwick Road Bridge. I will never forget the sight of Celtic fans, who had had a thoroughly 'happy' day out walking on the parapets of the bridge with the railway line beneath. But they weren't worried. Their team had done them proud.

As they headed back to the trains, Glasgow City Council dustbin lorries, Glasgow co-op milk carts, the odd ambulance and hearse, I realised I had been in the company of some of football's greatest fans.

What a great pity their world-famous club with its massive support across all the continents isn't competing in a more challenging environment today!! They and Rangers wouldn't half liven up the Premier League! As a result of which they would rapidly become major forces in Europe again as well as bringing their gigantic following with them everywhere.

21. The Man of God and Billy Bremner

In the seventies Leeds United had a reputation not only as a very powerful team but also one where many of their players were prepared to kick lumps out of their opponents to get a result. Billy Bremner was a fiery Scots midfielder, now with a statue in place at Elland Road in his memory. Away supporters standing near it are advised to wear shin pads!

How on earth Bremner stayed on the pitch whenever we played them the Lord only knows. Today he wouldn't get out of the tunnel!!!

The man who sat next to me that season in the Butler Street Stand at the Victoria Ground was a very devout and religious gentleman. He would quietly watch matches making calm and knowledgeable observations, ignoring the ranting and raving fans like me. He just sat there watching his beloved Stoke City and his favourite player, winger Terry Conroy.

It was nearing half time when Billy Bremner, who had already incited the Boothen End and everyone else with his over-aggressive attitude, hacked down TC as he was flying down the Butler Street wing.

Terry was really motoring and nearly finished up in the crowd in the Paddock on the half way line. It was the nearest thing to an attempted assassination seen at Stoke since time began. The Butler Street Paddock was about six feet below where we were sitting on the front row, a wooden planked wall separating us from those standing. Next thing we knew the religious gentleman was up on his feet and attempting to get into the Paddock. Then with his feet on the shoulders of the fans below he was screaming "I'll kill him, I'll kill him". He went absolutely bananas as Terry lay there in agony.

Fans around me and those below were wrestling with him as he tried to climb over their heads to get on the pitch to settle up with Billy. "I'll kill him, I'll Kill him!" he kept shouting.

Somehow, without help from Stoke-on-Trent Police, we all managed to get this mild-mannered man who had gone berserk back in his seat. He quickly regained his composure and returned to normal.

The following game he confided in me that he had said a special prayer of apology to the Lord at his Chapel, then told the Minister what he had been up to. And the Minister replied, "Pity you didn't manage to throttle him my son. He's been asking for it for years".

22. The Wind Sale - The Beginning of the End for Waddo. January 1976

The last place I wanted to be the night that Stoke City were due to play Spurs at home in an FA Cup Replay Tie in January 1976 was the famous Potters Club at Federation House, Stoke, opposite the railway station.

This club, the bastion of the British Pottery Manufacturers Federation, was a bit out of my league, but unfortunately my Manchester-based tile distribution company had called a management meeting there and despite my protests I had to miss the big match.

It was around 8.30pm when who should arrive at the Club but Stoke City Chairman Mr Albert Henshall and Tony Waddington, the City Manager. Needless to say, I wondered what on earth they were doing at the Potters Club during the middle of the match, so I quickly asked my boss if he wanted his drink topping up and went up to the bar where Mr Henshall and Tony were standing.

"I hope you don't mind me asking gentlemen, but why aren't you at the match?" I enquired.

Tony replied in a thoroughly fed up manner "Tell him Mr Chairman".

"I'm very sorry to say the roof has been blown off the Butler Street Stand and the match has been called off" the Chairman replied.

I was stunned and dumbfounded by the news.

"You've only told him half the story Mr Chairman. Tell him the other bad news because it will be all round the Potteries in the morning." Tony responded.

"We are under-insured so remedial action will be necessary by the Board to pay the bill."

I could not believe it and feared the worst. And I was right: Alan Hudson, Jimmy Greenhoff and Mike Pejic were all sold to pay the bill and our team was wrecked. The aftermath of all this is too painful to elaborate on, but our finest ever manager soon resigned and all the fans' dreams were destroyed.

23. Two Old Internationals Meet Again After 30 Years

When I saw my cricket team's fixtures for 1978 I realised we would be passing the Dog & Doublet pub in Sandon, near Stone, on our way back from an away match at Whitmore in North Staffordshire. The pub at that time was kept by a former Stoke City player, who many experts considered to be the finest ever in his position to play for England. The captain of my cricket team was also an ex-international and Derby County player and I knew they had both been in the England team in the late 1940s. On the way home, with my captain as a passenger in my car I suggested it might be pleasant to stop for a quick pint at the pub.

We walked in with our Skipper and the landlord behind his bar spotted him. He was absolutely stunned. "Wardy, Wardy. Good grief. Haven't seen you in years. What a surprise!". And the pair embraced.

The landlord was of course Stoke's legendary centre half Neil Franklin, and Tim Ward was the former England and Derby County player. Tim managed Carlisle, Grimsby Town, and Barnsley before taking on the Derby job and was the last manager before Brian Clough took over. He took all of them up except Derby where he couldn't get the Directors to spend a penny and left by mutual consent. I found out that Tim had been the manager of Barnsley when they played and murdered the Vale at Vale Park in the fifties. It was the day when Valiants legend Big Basil Hayward scored what was described at the time as the greatest headed goal ever seen on the ground. I saw it – the trouble was Bas put it in the back of his own net!!!

Neil along with Stoke winger George Mountford, who believe it or not kept Stanley Matthews out of the team at one time, were the first two English players to head to South America to play in Bogota, Columbia as the financial rewards were too great to resist. In England, the minimum wage was still in operation. The FA promptly banned Neil from playing for England. When Neil came home after a couple of years, he and George found their careers pretty well wrecked.

George did play a few games for Stoke as the club relented, but Neil left and finished at Hull City. Today Neil would have slotted beautifully into any Premier League side. They used to say about him that despite the muddy pitches he would finish the game with his white Stoke shorts spotlessly clean such was his poise and balance. Neil Franklin and Tim Ward - two immaculate, clean players who were both gentlemen and a credit to the game.

It was a pleasure to secretly plan their reunion.

24. Message from the Lord on Merseyside

In the late sixties, I used to find myself using the famous East Lancs Road, which connects Manchester and Liverpool, two or three times a week. One day I passed a church on the outskirts of Liverpool which had put up a huge sign saying, "What shall ye do when Christ comes to Liverpool?"

The next day I passed the church again and some bright spark had scrawled across it "Move St John to inside right!!"

For younger readers, Ian St John was the great Liverpool player.

25. The Champions

It was season 1977-8 and the mighty Liverpool were conquering Europe.

I was on business in Ipswich staying at the Copdock Hotel. As was customary I was having a few drinks with other people on business in the hotel bar. It was 9.30pm. We were all having a laugh and a joke. Suddenly a balding thickset individual came into the bar wearing a Liverpool FC tracksuit.

"Listen fellas, can you cool it a bit, the Champions of Europe are trying to get to sleep". It was Ronnie Moran, in his day a no-nonsense defender and Liverpool Manager, and later part of the famous Liverpool boot room under Bill Shankly.

We all quietly left the bar and went to bed having been given our orders. I can imagine what it must have been like playing for the Reds with Sergeant Moran dishing it out.

I opened my bedroom door the next morning and the door next to me opened at the same time. It was Crazy Horse, the great Liverpool captain Emlyn Hughes!

I had a few words with him and said I was a Stoke fan, and Emlyn, with that wonderful unforgettable adopted Scouse wit of his remarked, "Oh, you're one of the chip eaters, are you?"

Sadly, Emlyn passed away in 2004 at the age of 57, and Ronnie Moran died aged 83 the day before I wrote this tale in March 2017.

Two real Liverpool legends from those glory days when they really were the Champions of Europe.

26. Ex-Rams All Stars: Late '70s – Early '80s

In the late seventies and early eighties my wife and I were active supporters of the Ex-Rams All Stars, a team made up of old Derby County players, many of who had been members of the squad under the late great Brian Clough in 1972 when they won the old First Division and in 1975 when they won it again, this time under Dave Mackay.

Through our friendship with Tim Ward, the old Derby County and England player and former manager of the Club, we got to know many of those great retired players. And what lovely people they and their wives were. They made us feel really welcome. I am very proud as an ordinary Stoke supporter, just a face in the crowd as they say, to have had the pleasure of their company.

They were one hell of a team. They had to be to win the title twice in 1972 and 1975. Yes, they knew I was a Stokie and gave me a bit of stick, but I know they appreciated my wife's and my support.

One of the team, who I used to play cricket with and who had played in every single match in the two title-winning years - but who shuns publicity - once told me that because of the sheer motivational force of Brian Clough, when they ran out of the tunnel they knew they were going to win.

Tim organised the Ex-Rams team and the matches, which made thousands for charity in the Derby area. The Ex-Rams certainly brought the crowds in wherever they played.

It was a horrible, snowy Sunday afternoon in the depths of winter when we travelled with Tim and his charming wife Nancy to a 'friendly" against Moira Boys, a pit village team in north-west Leicestershire but a Derby County Stronghold. A mighty Ex-Rams team took the field including Alan Hinton, Archie Gemmill, Alan Durban, Kevin Hector and the finest centre half England had seen in years, the legendary Roy McFarland.

Tim as usual was on the touch line wearing his white Derby County number 6 shirt, acting as player manager. He was by this time a midfielder who was in his mid-fifties, and he rarely got a game such was the strength in depth of his squad. After ten minutes of uneventful play, with nothing happening to concern the Rams' defence Wardy suddenly held the Number 5 sub board up.

"Roy, Roy son, you're having a nightmare. I'm bringing you off".

Roy was absolutely flabbergasted at what happened next: guess who the sub was. Wardy. The old veteran couldn't wait to get out there as he clearly thought he would have a field day against mediocre opposition.

He'd replaced one of England's greatest ever centre halves so he could get a game himself, God Bless him.

27. And I Saw Nothing!! 8 November 1981

In the late seventies and early eighties I used to travel all over the Midlands with Tim Ward who was an official scout for his beloved Derby County, the club he had played for and managed.

Vale Park in the winter of the 1981-2 season for a Division Four game: the Valiants playing Rochdale was not particularly a match to look forward to. But Stoke were away that day, so at least this was a local game to watch. When we arrived, I was very proud to find myself sitting with Tim in the Directors' Box. But I was surprised to see many household names also in the Box, including Dave Sexton the former Manchester United Manager. I never asked Tim which player he was weighing up, and if I had asked him, for obvious reasons he would not have told me.

The match was played, from memory a dull 1-1 draw and I saw absolutely nothing to get excited about. All the players from what I could see were playing at their correct level and were likely to continue doing so.

Six months later my wife, Tim, his wife Nancy and I were watching a cricket match. Tim and I wandered off round the boundary and when we got back to the ladies my wife said "Rog, you won't believe what Nancy has just told me. Remember going to the Vale last winter with Tim? When he got home that night he spent the evening on the phone to the Directors and Manager of Derby County pleading with them sign a brilliant young winger who had been playing for the Vale that day".

I, as an ordinary fan, who always think I know better than the managers, saw nothing. As far as I was concerned it was a waste of 70 miles of Derby County's petrol. Fortunately for us, the Derby County Directors and Manager turned down Tim's advice. Within months the fabulous Mark Chamberlain was a Stoke City player, much to the fury of Vale fans, and again within months playing for England. And of course, his ability has been passed onto his son, Alex Oxlade-Chamberlain, the ex-Arsenal (now Liverpool) and England winger.

So, when 'know-alls' like me are ranting and raving, demanding a sub be brought on because one our lads is having a nightmare and needs carting off, remember these old pros like Tim see a totally different game to us. The eyes of experience of the game played - like Tim's - at the highest international level.

28. 'Bald Eagle' and Tarantini

Jim Smith the former football manager, known throughout the game as 'Bald Eagle' because of his totally bald bonce pulled off a real scoop transfer for Birmingham City in 1982. The Argentinian full back Tarantini, a full international signed to play for the Blues.

Unfortunately, he could not speak a word of English. Jim ordered a big blackboard for the dressing room and addressed the team. First with his white chalk he drew a goal with netting, then a foot and finally a football.

"Kick ball into goal " he said.

"Si - I understand Senor", Tarantini quickly responded.

To which the Bald Eagle, disparagingly surveying his team with glaring eyes, responded "I'm not talking to you son, I'm talking to this lot!!!"

29. The Trophy Winners - All Sold at Their Peak

Back in the late seventies and early eighties Stoke City's youth section was really flourishing and several lads broke into the first team and developed even faster than anticipated. All were sadly sold on for what was big money in those days, and all went on to win the highest honours in the domestic game as well as some European Trophies as well.

And what happened to us?

Yes, relegation in season 1984-5 which confirmed our worst fears that if you sell your best players you get what you deserve. It was 2008 before we returned to the top flight. Over 20 years in the wilderness.

I'm sorry to say, the feeling among the fans was that the Directors couldn't resist the temptation to cash in on these four talented and vital team players. And make a huge profit in the process. We, the fans, were just expected to put up with it, powerless to do anything but vote with our feet and stay away.

The first young star to be sold was local lad **Garth Crooks**, a lightning quick forward whose sheer pace terrified defenders. Sold in 1980 to Spurs for £650,000 (today's value c. £25million*)

Went on to win the following:

1980-1. FA Cup Winners Medal
1981-2. FA Cup Winners Medal
1983-4. UEFA Cup Winners Medal

AND TO THINK WE SOLD HIM

The second one sold was another local lad, **Adrian "Inchy" Heath** in 1981 for a club record fee of £750,000 to Everton (today's value c.£27million*). At the time Inchy had already made a name for himself as an attacking, goal-scoring forward. Once again, we cashed in and made a huge profit. Inchy went on to win the following with Everton:

1983-4. FA Cup Winners Medal
1984-5. Old First Division (now Premier League) Winners Medal
1986-7. Old First Division (now Premier League) Winners Medal

AND TO THINK WE SOLD HIM

Then in 1981-2 we sold a giant young centre forward who we had developed in the Club youth system, **Lee Chapman**, to our deadly enemies, the Arsenal of all people, for £500,000 (today's value c.£35million*). The fans' comments and the general abuse hurled at the Directors cannot be printed here. We couldn't believe it: yet again money ruled over the hearts of the Board. It didn't work out for Lee and he quickly moved for £400,000 to Leeds United. And guess what?

1988-9. League Cup Winners Medal
1991-2. Then the last ever old First Division Winners Medal

He scored 16 goals and was virtually unmarkable in the air. The following season saw the birth of the Premier League. The general feeling was that without him Leeds would probably not have won it.

AND TO THINK WE SOLD HIM

Finally, hard-working hard-tackling scheming midfielder **Paul Bracewell** was sold to Sunderland in 1983-4 for £250,000 (today's value c.£10m*). An absolute steal!! Then within a couple of seasons Everton snapped him up for £425,000. Yes, you've guessed it, more medals:

1983-4 Old First Division (now Premier League) Winners Medal
1984-5 UEFA Cup Winners Medal
In addition, Paul also played in four losing cup final sides.

AND TO THINK WE SOLD HIM

Is there a message here? Thankfully our owners now are Stoke City through and through.

"Today's values" are my own personal estimation of what I think they would get in today's market

30. The Return of Alan Hudson

In January 1984, playing in the old First Division, Stoke City were all over the place. It looked like we might be facing the dreaded drop. We could not put two passes together to save our lives, it was that grim. The players knew it, the fans knew it, and so did the directors and manager.

Oh, for someone to come back to rescue us in the way that Stanley Matthews had once.

We all knew there was only one player we wanted to sort it out. At a home match in January 1984 those sitting near the Directors' Box like me realised that one of our greatest ever players was present and the word spread round the Victoria Ground like wildfire. "He's here, he's here" and then at half time he was handed a microphone and booming over the loudspeaker a North London voice shouted to the crowd "How ya doing Boothen End? I'm coming back".

Our second greatest player ever, the one and only player who could sort it out. Yes, the talented, visionary, hard-working Alan Hudson.

The place went mad!!

The ball was passed to Alan from the kick off at his first match, which was at home. He put his foot on the ball, stopped dead still and beckoned with both hands to the opposition to "come and get it".

From that moment, he transformed us into a decent passing side and from the last 17 matches we amassed 34 points and stayed up.

That tells all you need to know about this incredibly gifted and wholehearted team player who always, repeat always, ran himself into the ground for us. A true Stoke City legend and a great star.

31. It's a Small World. Easter Saturday 1989

My wife's and my ceramic tile business in Burton upon Trent was very, very busy. It was Easter Saturday, traditionally one of the busiest days of the year for Home Improvement product dealers. Then in walked legendary former Derby County centre forward Jackie Stamps and his wife Nora. Both in their seventies, Jackie said "Roger lad, we've come to pick up our bathroom tile order".

Nora counted out the money, because the Big Man had sadly lost his sight in his fifties - many said through heading the old lace-up leather footballs, which when wet weighed half a ton. Jackie handed over the cash and I said to him "How are you going to get this lot home Jackie, because I know you and Nora haven't got a car?"

And Jackie replied in his brusque South Yorkshire accent "on that" and pointed to a Stevenson's double decker bus full of passengers waiting outside the showroom. I said "Jackie, it's not on a bus stop, there isn't one here".

He replied "Don't worry son, the drivers a pal of mine. He's had a word with the passengers and asked them if they are they happy about it and because it's me and Nora, they all agreed.

"Jackie, there are twenty-five square yards of tiles, four big buckets of Bal Tile Adhesive, a big bag of grout and six eight foot lengths of tile edging trim. You can't load that lot on the bus! I'll run you home with it all in my car", which I did.

When we arrived at Jackie and Nora's home we unloaded and Jackie said, "Put the kettle on Nora, Roger and I are going to talk football".

When I returned to our business one-and-a-half hours later, who should be sitting behind my desk, but Colin Boulton, the old Derby County goalie under Brian Clough, and who had won two First Division Champions medals in 1972 and in 1975 under Dave Mackay. Only a couple of years ago Colin was voted the Rams' all-time greatest goalkeeper by the fans.

Colin collected his order and left, and because my wife and I were having a long weekend in Abersoch in North Wales we knocked off early. We drove the three-and-a-half hour 150-mile journey to our hotel in Abersoch, opened the front door and walked straight into former Stoke City Manager Tony Waddington and his pal Potters director Mr Albert Henshall.

So many famous faces. All in one day, and 150 miles between them!!!

32. Jackie Stamps. Derby County legend

Jackie was built like a bulldozer and was a very competitive centre forward in the 1940s and early 1950s. He could dish it out and take it without any of today's histrionics. He scored 100 goals in 233 matches for his beloved Derby County.

My wife and myself got to know him quite well in his later years and when he died in November 1991 I had to attend a meeting at the North Stafford Hotel. It was on 20 November and that night the Vale had a big game at home against Liverpool in the League Cup. I was having a drink before the meeting surrounded by lots of Liverpool fans who were off to the game later. I told an elderly supporter that Jackie had passed away and he said "We remember Jackie well after the war when he played against us at Anfield. He was a real handful. Please tell his wife the Kopites send their love."

I did so, and Jackie's wife was totally overwhelmed.

That's the Football Family for you.

33. One Heart Attack Nearly Followed by Another

I was in intensive care in a Manchester hospital. It was in the early nineties.

I was recovering from a major heart attack and the subsequent operation and in the bed next to me was a Manchester City supporter with his blue and white scarf on. He had told the nurse that if he was going to snuff it he wanted to be wearing the club's colours.

We were obviously both very weak and feeling fragile. And then we learned what had happened at Selhurst Park, the home of Crystal Palace. Spectators at the match that day against Manchester United witnessed possibly the most memorable incident involving a player and a fan in the history of football. A Palace supporter had been giving the extrovert United star, Frenchman Eric Cantona, some stick. Unfortunately for the fan, Eric heard him and jumped feet first Kung-Fu style at him in the crowd. And he connected!! It was hilarious and while some fans were howling with rage, others were highly amused.

As you can imagine there was all hell let loose and Eric received a very lengthy suspension for his misdemeanour. When the City fan and I found out we started to laugh, and laugh, and laugh. We couldn't stop, despite being in such a frail state. It reached the stage where the intensive care duty nurse said to us "Do you realise you're both recovering from major heart surgery? If you are not careful you'll both have another one. Now you pair put a stop to it now". And then she too burst out laughing as well. She too was a Manchester City fan!!!

34. The President and the Barman

Mr Terry Shipman and his father Len before him were both Presidents of Leicester City. Terry and his wife, a couple of their best friends, and my wife and I became good holiday friends in the village of Los Gigantes, Tenerife.

Terry lived and breathed football. Often, we three men would pop into a local bar in the heat of the day, leaving the ladies on the sun-loungers around the hotel pool.

One day, when we arrived at our regular haunt, there was a new barman and he was wearing the famous Leicester City blue shirt with Club badge on it. He overheard us talking about football and about the Foxes and the Potters and promptly launched into a tirade of abuse about his team which was admittedly going through a bad patch. He railed on about the players, Manager, Directors and just about everything under the sun, saying it was a shambles and needed sorting out. He had no idea he was in the company of his club's President.

On the way back to the hotel I said to Terry "How on earth did you put up with that without saying anything?" And Terry replied "Rog, without the fans the game is nothing. They turn out in all weathers, when their team is having a bad run and the whole world and the ref seem against them, but they still follow them through thick and thin. It's in the blood. That's what it's all about and that's why we love football".

A room at Leicester City has recently been named the 'Shipman Suite' after Terry and his father. Father and son, football fans who gave their money and their all to the club they adored.

35. A Chance Encounter "Up 'Anley"

My wife and I were shopping in Hanley and as we climbed the outside steps to enter what is now Debenhams my wife said, "Rog, what's the matter? Are you okay? You've just stopped dead in your tracks".

"I've just felt a strange sensation. It really was most peculiar, "I replied.

We looked to our left and no more than a yard away a spritely elderly gentleman in a smart grey tracksuit, trainers and baseball cap was nipping up the steps.

Despite all my years watching Stoke City, it was the closest I ever came to Sir Stanley Matthews, who was quietly going about his business among his own people. And then he was gone, just mingling in with the shopping crowds.

The feeling I had that day remains with me still whenever the man who gave football to so much of the world is mentioned.

36. Sir Stanley Matthews' Funeral, 3 March 2000

For health and work reasons I had been unable to attend Stoke matches for 14 long years. A major heart attack and Saturday working in our own ceramic tile business in Burton put football way down the priority list for obvious reasons, although I still followed the Potters through the media. My wife and I were in the process of retiring and closing down our business when I heard of Sir Stanley Matthews' death, at the Nuffield Hospital in Clayton. After the initial shock, the memories came flooding back, and when I learned of the Great Man's funeral date I had to be there.

On the morning of the funeral I arrived in the Potteries after my 30-odd mile journey from home and parked in Hartshill, as I had done so often in bygone years when attending Potters matches. It was a bitterly cold morning with episodic hailstorms. As I made my way on foot to the now desolate Victoria Ground around 9.30am, I could not believe how many people were heading in the same direction, some young, some middle-aged, and the veterans, many with walking sticks. Both male and female being drawn to the old ground. It was like a pilgrimage. No, it WAS a pilgrimage.

I stood outside the old Supporters' Club and surveyed the scene. I could see the remains of the lower steps of the Boothen End covered in grass and mud, and this barren area which once was our Football Chapel of Dreams. On what was the old centre circle, fans had erected a large upright board. People were walking up to it, many placing notes of commiseration and commemoration on the board and surrounding it with wreaths and club scarves. By 10.00am thousands and thousands of fans had arrived to pay tribute. Because of the sheer numbers, I realised that if I was going to get anywhere near St Peter's Church in Stoke, about half a mile from the ground, I needed to get a move on. I managed to get about 50-60 yards away from the entrance to the church where already hundreds and hundreds of people had arrived. You could hear a pin drop if it hadn't been for the whirring of the media's helicopter blades above. There were young children on their fathers' shoulders, young fans not old enough to have seen Sir Stan play and the older ones for who this was a very emotional day. What struck me was the exemplary behaviour of the youngsters. They realised I think that they were witnessing a sad moment in the history of our national game and of the Potteries.

Then buses started to arrive from football clubs all over the United Kingdom. Blackpool of course, and so many others. As the service began, with thousands packed in outside, loudspeakers relayed to us the proceedings and tributes. And in the middle of it all there was an enormous hailstorm. Everyone continued to stand bolt upright and in respectful silence. We were all soaked to the skin but not one person budged. Everyone was determined to see it through. The service ended and as Sir Stan's coffin was brought out on the shoulders of some of the greatest players of all time, the hailstorm stopped and the sun came out. There was a huge gasp from us all. It was a strange, strange happening and I think everyone was stunned by it. It was truly uncanny.

It was only when I arrived home and was watching the massive coverage on television that I realised I had attended such a huge occasion. As Sir Stan's coffin was driven through the streets of our City, it was estimated to be the largest turnout for a funeral, outside the Royal Family, for anyone since Winston Churchill.

And now Sir Stan, your memory lives on through The Sir Stanley Matthews Coaching Foundation of which I am proud, as a man of the Potteries, to be an Ambassador.

37. Day Out in the Directors' Box at the "Blue Camp"

Stoke City had been drawn away against Manchester City in the FA Cup, and a pal of mine who knows the Man City legend Mike Summerbee quite well asked me if I would like to go with him. My pal was not the slightest bit interested in football – he's a big Leicester Tigers rugby fan. But through Mike he kindly arranged to secure tickets for the game.

Imagine my surprise when I found myself being royally entertained in the Directors' Box and Executive Suite. Me, just an ordinary fan, who travels on the free coaches to away games with the Potters and sits and stands like all of us do cheering the lads on. Bedecked in my Stoke City red and white scarf, I stood out like a sore thumb.

When my wife and I had lived in leafy North Cheshire in the late sixties and early seventies we met many Manchester City supporters and I realised then that they were a bit like us. Like true fans, through the good times and the bad, they had stuck with their home town team. Any success was a bonus. Although a much bigger club with a fan base twice as big as ours, I felt at ease with the City fans.

Now of course, with the huge financial backing they have the bar is set a lot higher. But when I was in that Directors' Suite and Box they were still the same old Manchester City people, called the Noisy Neighbours by their local rivals Manchester United. It wasn't a full house, but our fans kicked up a hell of a racket and we earned a replay. After the match, the hospitality I received from everyone - from the stewards, the waitresses and the executives in the Directors' Suite area - was unbelievable. They were, every one of them, absolutely super to me. And then, all of a sudden, a huge hand appeared and a voice said, "I'm Tommy Booth, welcome to City."

Tommy was a fine midfield player in the legendary City teams of the Seventies. I was gobsmacked when he then said, "I'd like to introduce you to Tony Book, our skipper in those days." And then, to cap it all, I met possibly City's greatest ever player, Colin Bell, who manager Joe Mercer had nicknamed Nijinsky after the famous racehorse because he was so quick!! And this on top of being with the late Georgie Best's great pal Mike Summerbee and his charming wife and daughter.

I have attended many matches at City's cavernous old stadium Maine Road, which once held over 84,000 fans for a cup tie against the Potters in 1934. The largest ever English gate outside Wembley.

Until that day I had never been to a match at City's new Etihad ground, nicknamed the "Blue Camp". I can only say the warm welcome from everyone at this fine old majestic football club will remain with me for ever. Their Club Anthem "Blue Moon" sums them up.

38. A "Neck-Ender" in Paradise

After the terrific win against Manchester City in November 2015, when Stoke City was being described as "Stokealona" my wife and I were on holiday in Madeira. It's our little bit of paradise.

Madeira's capital, the city of Funchal, is a relaxed genteel resort. Cars stop at pedestrian crossings, and you rarely hear a car horn. The Madeiran people speak politely and quietly and an atmosphere of peaceful serenity pervades the place.

They call the Island "the waiting room" as the main visitors tend to be elderly. The winter in Madeira is known as "the season of the ships" as it is a very popular port of call for the massive cruise ships from northern Europe bringing people to warmer climes. It's also the last port before crossing the Atlantic bound for the West Indies, the USA, or Brazil and South America.

Overlooking the city and harbour is the world-famous Reid's Hotel, with its clientele of very wealthy individuals and film stars. Afternoon tea at Reid's is an absolute number one target for the ladies. People wearing football shirts are pretty well unheard of.

My wife and I were walking up the hill on the road just before Reid's when guess what? A man bedecked in the famous red and white Stoke City shirt and a blue weather-worn Club cap was marching down the hill. He was beaming with pride, chest stuck out and generally looked a very happy character.

As we approached each other outside Reid's he spotted my Sir Stanley Matthews Coaching Foundation badge on my shirt which I wear at all times. "Ay up", he said "What a win against City. Where are you from? I'm from the Estate at Neck End".
"We're thirty miles down the road from the Brit, near Burton, but Potteries born and bred" I replied.
"Tell you what pal" he said, "I'm flipping starving. Shall we have a chat and see if they - pointing to Reid's - have got Oatcakes on the menu?"

My wife then forcibly intervened. "If you think I'm going in there with you pair with him dressed like that, you've got another think coming!!!"

And that, as they say, was the end of that.

"Neck End" is the nickname for the Meir area in Stoke-on-Trent.

39. Away at the Baggies

January 2016. I hadn't been to an away game at West Brom for years. As usual, when I travel away I use the free coaches which Stoke City make available. A wonderful gesture of thanks by the Board to the fans.

We off-loaded at West Brom and as always, I looked out for a well-known elderly Stoke fan nicknamed Zig - many of you will know the gentleman concerned. I think he attends every game, and everywhere we go the stewards seem to know him. So, I carried out my customary tactic of following him as he always knows the quickest way to any ground.

Because I had been suffering from a bad leg I was using my grandfather's walking stick, and as I followed Zig and many other fans up a very steep hill I said to him near the top, with my leg in agony, "Flipping heck Zig this is a hell of a climb. I know the Hawthorns is one of the highest grounds in the country, but not this high".

Zig responded "We aren't going to the ground up here duck. We're going to Morrisons to fetch our dinners. THE GROUND'S DOWN THERE at the bottom around the corner."

40. Destiny Day at Doncaster

Doncaster Rovers v Burton Albion on a blazing hot day in May 2016.

I can only describe it as an absolute nightmare to watch, and my wife and I are Stokies! I was there with my wife supporting a town's football team, a club whose matches we rarely attended, being Stoke City fans.

Burton, the town in whose vicinity we had lived for forty-three years, needed a point to win promotion to the Championship. Walsall, playing at Port Vale, were breathing down their necks. If the Albion lost and Walsall won it would all end in tears.

We had to be there to support the town that had given my wife and I our living. So, we travelled with friends who are Forest fans on one of the official coaches the Club laid on.

It was a quiet journey as the convoy headed up the A38, the M1 and then over to Doncaster. Supporters on our coach were near nervous wrecks before they even got to the ground. Just the journey, only about one hour fifteen minutes, was a real endurance test.

A few fans on the coach tried to liven things up with the occasional joke, but no one was listening. They were lost in a world of their own, dreading the dream of promotion being denied them. As we got off the coaches, all around us it was like a carnival. The Town and The Albion were going to have a good day out regardless.

And boy oh boy they did!!!

Many of the three thousand plus fans were in fancy dress and they sang and danced as they marched to the stadium. A kaleidoscope of colour and an explosion of noise as they raised the rafters in their seats.

"Everything will be alright" was rendered time and time again before and during the match until horrific news broke on mobiles that Walsall were winning, first one nil, then two nil, and then unbelievably three nil at Vale Park at half time.

Albion fans around us behind one of the goals were in a dreadful state. 'The Brewers' had not played badly in the first half, but they had not played particularly well either. Most importantly though they had not conceded, so it was nil nil at the interval.

With Walsall looking like having the vital three points in the bag, if Burton conceded a goal and lost then everything was "down the pan", which is probably a suitable description of the state of the fans' and Chairman's backsides for those fateful forty-five minutes in the second half. Somehow, they came through it and secured that vital draw and promotion to the Championship.

From non-league football to one of the strongest leagues in Europe and all so quickly. Non-league in 2008 to playing Derby County, Forest, The Villa, Newcastle United, Birmingham City, Leeds United and the Wolves. All huge clubs with enough away support to fill the Pirelli Stadium themselves.

A club with gates rarely exceeding 4,000 at the time and with their spanking new stadium only holding 6,800.

My Wife and I had the pleasure of sitting next to the Albion Chairman Ben Robinson at a lunch recently. We have known each other for donkey's years having both established our businesses in Burton in the mid-eighties only four hundred yards from each other. I commented to Ben that my wife and I had been at Doncaster that fateful day.

"Rog" Ben said "The last twenty minutes were the worst of my forty years in football" You can say that again Mr Chairman!!!

As "just a face in the crowd" that day, the sheer look of disbelief of elderly Burton Albion fans told the story and will live with me forever. Those veteran fans who sometimes in the early years of this century numbered under 1,000 at home games at the old Eton Park Ground. Truly one of football's all-time fairy stories.

41. Good Morning Mr President

Arriving at a garage in the Potteries not too long ago following yet another wrecked tyre caused by potholes, my wife nudged me and said "Rog, you won't believe who is sitting over there in the waiting area".

I turned and saw an elderly gentleman sitting quietly all on his own enjoying a coffee. I had to go over to speak to him. I was as usual wearing my weather-worn blue Stoke City cap.

"Good morning Mr President" I said to England's greatest ever goalie, Gordon Banks.

And for the next fifty minutes Gordon, my wife and I just chatted away about everything under the sun. FIFTY MINUTES with a true legend.

It was an unforgettable experience to meet one of the most unassuming, and modest individuals we have been fortunate enough to have a conversation with in all our lives. We are so proud to have met him.

The Stoke City President and always "Banks of England".

42. Zigger-Zagger-Zigger-Zagger-Stoke-City. John Bayley

These days, and now well into his seventies, truly exceptional Stoke City fan John Bayley holds court sitting on a wall – known as "The Wall of Fame" - by the Club shop on home match days.

He is always surrounded by a crowd of veterans who have a word with him, like me, before moving onto our seat in the bet365 Stadium.

There are forever arguments raging at the wall about incidents in matches going back over sixty years.

The old timers like me revel in it. We are all a band of know-alls.

But when push comes to shove as we say, one person has a distinct advantage over everyone else. He was there, he saw it in the flesh!!! Home or away, and hardly missing a game during those sixty long years, one season he even attended every Reserve match too, home and away!!!

Unbelievable devotion to his Club.

Zig, whose blood bleeds red and white, is our most well-known fan.

To have a play written about him 'Zigger-Zagger' is quite something, but has it changed him? Not one little bit. He just mingles in among his family of Stokies. Younger fans will have heard of him, but will not know much about his history.

In the sixties when massed standing crowds started chanting and singing in unison on the huge terraces on the Kop at Anfield; the Shed End at the Bridge; Goodison; the Stretford End; the Gallowgate at St James Park; Roker; the Holte Lane End at the Villa; the North Bank at the Arsenal; and of course, the Boothen End, it was Zig who led the way with the Stoke fans.

"Zigger-Zagger-Zigger-Zagger-Stoke-Citee!!"

Today John has mellowed somewhat, but still leads us, particularly at away matches.

He now acts as a helper on the free away coaches, advising fans of places of interest on the journey. He like a tour guide!!

And then when we are getting near the away ground in question, whether it's St. Marys, the Stadium of Light, the Emirates, or Old Trafford he knows all the short cuts for the bus driver to take.

Off-loading at the ground it is amazing how many of the home stewards know him and because of his new hip he tends to get preferential treatment.

I only met John for the first time a couple of years ago, but I'll tell you what, he certainly knows his football and of course his cricket, where he's a keen supporter of North Staffs League Cricket club Longton and the County Team as well.

Years ago, Zig finished sixth in a national competition to find football's most devoted fan. Today, he'd walk it!!

Well done John and long may you continue to follow the team you love, but please don't finish up in a scrap with a fellow Stokie OAP about an offside decision years ago at a Reserve match!!

43. The Real Football Fairy Story of This Century

Whilst Leicester City in 2016 won all the plaudits from the press for their remarkable Premiership-winning season, quietly a small town's football club in the back woods of East Staffordshire was producing truly one of the greatest fairy tales in the history of English Football.

Surrounded by Derby County, Nottingham Forest, Leicester City, Aston Villa, Birmingham City, the Wolves, West Brom and Stoke City, all within 45 minutes' journey, little Burton Albion who only eight years ago were playing non-league football, not only worked their way through the lower leagues to the Championship in 2016, in 2017 they unbelievably managed to stay up.

With attendances often barely exceeding 4,000 it was only the massive away support of clubs like Newcastle United, the Villa, Leeds United, Sheffield Wednesday, plus visits from Derby County, Birmingham City and Notts Forest that boosted the average attendance to around 5,000 for the season.

And even then, for most of these huge fixtures the capacity of around just under 7,000 was not reached. The next lowest average was at Rotherham United with almost double the attendance figure.

Running the club on a shoestring under the astute Chairmanship of local businessman Ben Robinson, and with the vastly experienced Nigel Clough as Manager for the second time, the pair dovetailed wonderfully.

Even with Ben as Chairman with all those years of tough non-league football behind him; and Nigel Clough, the son of arguably the greatest ever English manager the incomparable Brian Clough, as Manager, the bookies, the national press and pretty well every football fan wrote them off as relegation cannon fodder. Doomed without a cat in Hell's chance!!!

Nigel had spent several seasons previously at the Albion bringing them through to the verge of football league status before Derby County recruited him. An offer he could not resist. Then a succession of managerial jobs with clubs in the Football League where he lacked financial support to succeed.

A battle-hardened boss who knew that with team spirit and 100 per cent support from his team's dressing room anything was possible.

Nigel, like his father before him, instilled into his Burton Albion players the sheer motivation to realise the impossible. Every time they ran out onto the pitch they knew they could do it!

And survive they did, with any number of on loan players and run of the mill lower league professionals seeing them through to another season in arguably one of the most competitive leagues in world football.

The population of Burton upon Trent is around 75,000. Yes, only 75,000. Many of them are dyed-in-the-wool Derby County fans, as well as the Villa and other major clubs in the area. 'Like father like son', it's almost impossible to persuade them to give up their family's club, which they've been following in many cases for generations. But the hardcore Burton support - going back to non-league days, and games against deadly rivals Gresley Rovers - will always be there. But there are only around 1,500 to 2,000 of them. The rest are known as fair weather supporters who will probably never be seen again if results go the wrong way. The real fans, several of whom I know, are in seventh heaven with trips to Newcastle United, Leeds United, Derby County and the Villa under their belt and points gained. Each morning they wake up and think "Is this really happening, or is it a dream?

No, it isn't a dream. Pinch yourselves you Albion Supporters. Against all the odds you not only got there, you survived. You lived to fight another day.

Along with thousands of fans nationwide like me, a Stokie, we will be looking out for your result on our way home from our match and asking, "How've the Albion gone on today?"

And if they've earned a hard-earned point away at Sunderland, Leeds United, The Villa and the "Rams" we will say to ourselves, "Bring em on you Brewers!"

Truly one of the most memorable and romantic stories in football.

44. Claim to Fame

My late Father, brought up in Etruria Vicarage from 1914, when my Grandfather arrived as the Vicar and remained there until his death in the late fifties reckons he was the only man of his age in the Six Towns and Newcastle NEVER to have met or played with or against Sir Stanley Matthews.

But Sir Stan was still his hero!!

45. The Newsagent

When my wife and I left the Potteries in 1967 to live at Poynton in "leafy" North Cheshire, as Annie Walker, landlady of the Rover's Return on Coronation Street used to call the area, little did I realise I was moving into such cauldron of football rivalry.

And it's still as bad today, with even the local ladies dress shop called Blues. Yes, Poynton is a hotbed of Manchester City fans including our former friends and neighbours from fifty years ago - with whom we have remained in close contact, despite leaving the area in 1973 to live in East Staffordshire.

The atmosphere in Manchester in the late sixties and early seventies was dominated by football as it still is today. There was and is no escape from it. For me as a Stoke fan it was hilarious to listen to the banter.

The Newsagent in the village was owned by a United-mad fan named Bob so you can imagine when United won and City lost on the same day he was on top of the world and couldn't wait to search out City fans. The paper boys delivered the Manchester Evening News each night to many houses, but those properties owned by City fans would get a personal delivery from Bob. Yes, he knew exactly where they lived and couldn't wait to torment them. He used to ring the bell, bang on the door time after time and even the front window until they appeared on the doorstep.

City supporters, even in the early Autumn and Spring when it was reasonably light decided there was only one solution. They drew the curtains and ignored him. He would then not deliver the paper so they had no choice but to go and fetch it the next morning where a beaming Bob would be waiting to give them "some stick".

As a Stokie in the middle of all this my wife and I got the same treatment too if the Potters were beaten and United had won, which sadly was far too often. Those six years until we left in 1973 were an unforgettable experience for me as a football fanatic. I loved every minute of it, and when we return to the area visiting our friends, I still look at that newsagents with great affection and the memories of a football-mad area come flooding back.

Living on the edge of the great City of Manchester and travelling for six years throughout the northwest including Merseyside where the rivalry between Everton and Liverpool fans was and still is as fierce as ever, it gave me an insight of just what football means to so many hundreds of thousands of lovers of the game. As Bill Shankly, the immortal Liverpool Manager once said, "Some people think football is a matter of life or death. I can assure them it's far more important than that."!!